Theological Reflection

Theological Reflection

Connecting Faith and Life

Catholic Basics
A Pastoral Ministry Series

Joye Gros, O.P., D.Min.

Thomas P. Walters, Ph.D.
Series Editor

NATIONAL CONFERENCE FOR
CATECHETAL LEADERSHIP

LOYOLAPRESS.
3441 N. ASHLAND AVENUE
CHICAGO, ILLINOIS 60657

NIHIL OBSTAT: Rev. Daniel J. Mahan, S.T.B., S.T.L.
Censor Librorum

IMPRIMATUR: Rev. Msgr. Joseph F. Schaedel
Vicar General/Moderator of the Curia

Given at Indianapolis, Indiana, on February 19, 2001

The *nihil obstat* and *imprimatur* are official declarations that a book is free of doctrinal and moral error. No implication is contained herein that those who have granted the *nihil obstat* and *imprimatur* agree with the content, opinions, or statements expressed.

Acknowledgments appearing on p. 67 constitute a continuation of the copyright page.

Cover Design: Other Brother Design
Cover Illustration: Steven Snodgrass
Interior Illustration: Other Brother Design

Library of Congress Cataloging-in-Publication Data

Gros, Joye.
    Theological reflection : connecting faith and life / Joye Gros.
        p. cm. – (Catholic basics)
    Rev. ed. of: Connecting faith and life.
    Includes bibliographical references.
    ISBN 0-8294-1724-9
    1. Pastoral theology–Catholic Church–Meditations. I. Gros, Joye.
Connecting faith and life. II. Title. III. Series.

BX1913 .G75 2001
230'.2–dc21   2001029695
                                                           CIP

ISBN: 0-8294-1724-9

    04   05   Bang 5   4   3

TABLE OF CONTENTS

About the Series   vii

Certification Standards: National Resources for
    Church Ministry   viii

Preface   x

Introduction   xi

CHAPTER 1: THEOLOGICAL REFLECTION: THE
WHAT AND THE WHY   1

Theological Reflection: A Natural Activity   3

The Potential for Transformation   5

For Reflection   6

CHAPTER 2: THEOLOGICAL REFLECTION: THE
MODEL   7

Experience   8

Tradition   11

Culture   12

For Reflection   14

CHAPTER 3: THEOLOGICAL REFLECTION: THE
METHOD   16

Attending   17

Asserting   19

Decision Making   21

For Reflection   22

CHAPTER 4: THEOLOGICAL REFLECTION:
HOW TO BEGIN   23

Rite of Christian Initiation of Adults   24

Faith-Sharing Group   27

Religious Education Class   31

For Reflection   33

CHAPTER 5: THEOLOGICAL REFLECTION: THE
FACILITATOR   35

You as the Facilitator   36

Gaining Clarity About Feelings   38

Staying with the Experience   40

Guidelines for Faith Sharing   41

Framing the Questions   43

Challenges and Gifts Within a Group   45

For Reflection   47

CHAPTER 6: THEOLOGICAL REFLECTION: THE
DISCIPLINE OF AUTHENTICITY   48

Facilitators Serve as Formed and Informed Resources   49

Facilitators Are Deep Listeners   50

Facilitators Are Faithful to the Tradition   50

Attending to Preparation   51

For Reflection   54

CHAPTER 7: THEOLOGICAL REFLECTION:
WHAT'S IT TO ME?   56

Reciprocity: The Nature of Ministry   59

For Reflection   61

Abbreviations   62

Bibliography   63

Recommended Resources   65

Acknowledgments   67

About the Author   68

About the Series

Catholic Basics: A Pastoral Ministry Series offers an in-depth yet accessible understanding of the fundamentals of the Catholic faith for adults, both those preparing for lay ministry and those interested in the topics for their own personal growth. The series helps readers explore the Catholic tradition and apply what they have learned to their lives and ministry situations. Each title offers a reliable introduction to a specific topic and provides a foundational understanding of the concepts.

Each book in the series presents a Catholic understanding of its topic as found in Scripture and the teachings of the Church. Each of the authors has paid special attention to the documents of the Second Vatican Council and the *Catechism of the Catholic Church*, so that further learning can be guided by these core resources.

Chapters conclude with study questions that may be used for small group review or for individual reflection. Additionally, suggestions for further reading offer dependable guides for extra study.

The initiative of the National Conference of Catechetical Leadership led to the development of an earlier version of this series. The indispensable contribution of the series editor, Dr. Thomas Walters, helped ensure that the concepts and ideas presented here are easily accessible to a wide audience.

CERTIFICATION STANDARDS: NATIONAL RESOURCES FOR CHURCH MINISTRY

E ach book in this theology series relates to standards for theological competency identified in the resources listed below. Three national church ministry organizations provide standards for certification programs that serve their respective ministries. The standards were developed in collaboration with the United States Catholic Conference Commission on Certification and Accreditation. The fourth resource is the latest document, developed to identify common goals of the three sets of standards.

Competency Based Certification Standards for Pastoral Ministers, Pastoral Associates and Parish Life Coordinators. Chicago: National Association for Lay Ministry, Inc. (NALM), 1994.

These standards address three roles found in pastoral ministry settings in the United States. They were the earliest to receive approval from the United States Catholic Conference Commission on Certification and Accreditation. Copies are available from the National Association for Lay Ministry, 5420 S. Cornell, Chicago, IL 60615-5604.

National Certification Standards for Professional Parish Directors of Religious Education. Washington, DC: National Conference for Catechetical Leadership, 1998.

NCCL developed standards to foster appropriate initial education and formation, as well as continuing personal and professional development, of those who serve as directors of religious education (DREs). The standards address various areas of knowledge and abilities needed in the personal, theological, and professional aspects of the ministry. Also included is a code of ethics for professional catechetical leaders. Available from the National Conference of Catechetical Leadership, 3021 Fourth Street NE, Washington, DC 20017-1102.

NFCYM Competency-Based Standards for the Coordinator of Youth Ministry. Washington, DC: National Federation for Catholic Youth Ministry, 1996.

This document lays out the wide range of knowledge and skills that support ministry with young people, as well as the successful leadership and organization of youth ministry wherever it may be situated. The standards are available from the National Federation for Catholic Youth Ministry, 415 Michigan Avenue NE, Suite 40, Washington, DC 20017-1518.

Merkt, Joseph T., ed. *Common Formation Goals for Ministry.* A joint publication of NALM, NFCYM, and NCCL, 2000.

Rev. Joseph Merkt compared the documentation of standards cited by three national organizations serving pastoral, youth, and catechetical ministries. The resulting statement of common goals identifies common ground for those who prepare persons for ministry, as well as for the many who wear multiple hats. Copies are available from NALM, NCCL, or NFCYM.

Preface

I first recognize my brother, Jeff Gros, FSC, who got me into this project. He recommended me to Tom Walters, the series editor, and thus began this journey of articulating a sacred process. Next I thank Margaret Rose Curry, OP, who tediously and tirelessly edited every comma, phrase, and sentence structure. Jean Bohr, D Min, watched for clarity and content flow, and encouraged me each and every step along the way. Barbara Flynn, Lois McGovern, OP, and Teresa Tuite, OP, began with encouragement and support and didn't let up until I finished. I have been blessed with cheerleaders, coaches, and confidence builders. Last, but certainly not least, I thank Tom Walters, who provided the framework and direction to keep me on track. This has, indeed, been a blessed journey. May those who read and reflect on this book be graced by the same sacred stirrings that have given birth to this endeavor. We do know the Source of life and creativity. It was a pleasure to partner in the dance of creation.

Introduction

Several years ago friends of mine gave me snorkeling equipment to take on my vacation. I hesitated, as the flippers, hoses, and face masks were cumbersome and awkward to pack. I could not imagine that anything as interesting as snorkeling would require such inconvenience. It seemed a great deal of trouble just to put my face in the water! Wouldn't plain old goggles do?

Perhaps it was because my friends were so convincing about the fun of snorkeling or, more likely, because I did not know how to say no in the face of their generosity—whatever the reason, I packed the equipment. It sat in the hotel room for several days, however, because I just didn't want to haul it to the beach each day. I had towels, chairs, incrementally graded sunscreen, books, hats, the ever-present water bottle, and so on.

Then one day there was an offer: A boat would take me offshore to snorkel. I would be given equipment, taught the technique, and taken into deep coastal waters which offered incredible underwater vistas. Well, I thought, if I am going to do this at all, I probably should learn how.

My friend and I climbed aboard a tour boat, and off we went into the wild blue ocean. Fitted with fins and face masks, we learned the basics of breathing in the mask. We were taught how to get in and out of the boat and told what we might see. I adjusted my equipment, descended the ladder, and positioned myself for my first look.

I was startled! I was amazed! I was in awe! It was like looking into a huge tropical fish aquarium. I was caught between wanting to surface to say, "Wow! Look at that!" and wanting to stay transfixed to the technicolor show that was taking place before my very eyes.

Needless to say, the gear got used! I was converted. I was transformed. I was a "preacher" of the "good news" of snorkeling!

Each day we would go to the beach at sunset. I could spend hours just looking at the horizon and marveling at the beauty, its constancy, and its flow. And I never forgot what I learned from snorkeling: No matter how beautiful the surface is—and it is—looking beneath it reveals a whole new world. Its beauty and depth is invisible to the eye unless you take the time, put your face in the water, and take a gander. If you do, you are gifted with incredible sight and insight!

For me, snorkeling has become an image of theological reflection—the attempt to see deeply into life experiences. Theological reflection provides the framework that helps us see the connection between the surface and the depths of life's meanings. It encourages us to recognize the intimate connection between faith and daily life.

Many people today are asking the "meaning-making" questions. We want our lives to have meaning. We want to know how our faith informs our work life, how our family life enhances our spirituality, and how we can feel less fragmented and more whole. These are the spiritual questions of life. They are wisdom-seeking invitations stirring within the depths of our souls. These are the hungers that theological reflection can help feed.

We know the experience of fragmentation into a work life, a family life, a leisure life, and a faith life. We often feel divided by these distinctions and separations, and we long for integration. Theological reflection is a model and method that will assist us in that process of integration.

This book offers an understanding of theological reflection—a model and a method. It will not only illustrate how readers may use theological reflection in their own spiritual development but will also show how to facilitate the process with others. My hope is that as you look at the horizon of your life, you may know, too, the reality of its depths, and you will take the opportunity to look deeply. So let's go snorkeling!

CHAPTER 1

Theological Reflection: The What and the Why

Jump In! The Water's Fine: A' Snorkeling We Will Go!

What is theological reflection, and why would we want to do it? It can sound so lofty, so complicated, so ominous. It sounds like something meant for "religious types," not everyday people. At the same time, it is intriguing. It has a pull, a lure. It draws us. While I was studying the art and skill of theological reflection, my teacher and mentor, John (Jack) Shea, would begin a class with what appeared to be a simple question: "So, what's happening out there?" Someone in the class would relate something that had happened, usually in the form of a story. From there the session would continue with what appeared to be a normal discussion, but at the end of class we would realize that we were in a different reflective space than at the beginning. Through Jack's questions and comments, and the interaction of the group, we came into contact with some of our beliefs, how shared experiences affected those beliefs, and how those very beliefs shed light on the story.

I remember asking Jack, "How do you do that?" He laughed and said, "You do it too." As much as I wanted to believe him, I was skeptical. Being an educator by profession, I wanted a step-by-step approach, perhaps even a lesson plan! Instead, Jack led our class to understand the experience and dynamics of theological reflection before we learned the "how-to's."

Several years later, I ran into Jack at the University of St. Mary of the Lake Seminary in Mundelein, Illinois. At the time I was facilitating a small group of seminarians in the process of theological reflection. The men had been working in parishes for a semester of their field education and had returned to the seminary to gather in small groups and reflect on their experiences in light of the Christian tradition. One day Jack asked how the group was going. I said, "It's great. I love it. They've got it, but they just don't know it yet!" Jack, remembering my anxiety about "getting it," leaned his head back and laughed. We both remembered.

Theological Reflection: A Natural Activity

Theological reflection is a natural activity; we do it all the time. It gives us a feeling of congruence and depth, even in the midst of difficult situations. It deepens meaning and it happens naturally, but if we could do it intentionally and spontaneously, it would enrich our ministry and our lives. It is a discipline and, like any discipline, it requires practice and attention to become a natural part of us.

Theological reflection is a tool or means that helps us reflect in ways that allow faith to touch our lives and our lives to touch our faith. So often we can feel as though our lives are fragmented. Religion belongs in church—or at least at parish functions, at grace before and after meals, and at prayer in times of sickness or fear. But what does religion have to do with my everyday life? What connection does "churchy" stuff have to the problems and joys of the home, the workplace, and the leisure space?

Theological reflection is an attempt to integrate the segments of our lives so that we can live and breathe our beliefs. Theological reflection is believing that our everyday living is an important agenda for our faith and that our faith has a voice in our everyday life. It's an activity of integration. It's an activity of reciprocity. In our ancient tradition this would have been called searching for wisdom and at the same time growing in wisdom.

In their book titled *The Art of Theological Reflection*, Patricia O'Connell Killen and John de Beer define theological reflection as:

> . . . the discipline of exploring individual and corporate experience in conversation with the wisdom of a religious heritage. The conversation is a genuine dialogue that seeks to hear from our own beliefs, actions, and perspectives, as well as those of the tradition. It respects the integrity of both. Theological reflection, therefore, may confirm, challenge, clarify, and expand how we understand

our own experience and how we understand the religious tradition. The outcome is new truth and meaning for living. (p. viii)

In *The Book of Sacramental Basics*, Tad Guzie points out the difference between raw experience and lived experience. All experience is raw until it is reflected upon. Theological reflection makes raw experience into lived experience and moves an individual from insight to action.

So often we hear people express a desire for meaning in their lives. At the same time they are faced with multiple demands on their time. If we pay attention to current best-selling books, contemporary music, and talk-show themes, we would notice again and again the quest for depth, the hunger for spirituality. People often see the holy as "other," or at least "other worldly." The Second Vatican Council, however, and the *Catechism of the Catholic Church (CCC)* re-echo our baptismal call to holiness (*CCC*, #1279, 1280). We are all called to holiness, and that holiness is not separate from our everyday lives. It is our desire and our fear, our lure and our resistance. We long for holiness—and we are uneasy about it. Part of the disease resides in our images of the holy: what a holy person would look like, what it would require of me, how others would treat me, and so on.

Perhaps the longing for holiness is the desire to recognize the divine in everyday life, to trust in the mystery of the Incarnation, to recognize our God as both immanent and transcendent (see *CCC*, #51–53). God is within us and without, in our midst yet beyond us. This Absolute and Infinite Being is present to creation at all times for "in him we live and move and have our being" (Acts 17:28). The ambivalent and embracing nature of God both lures and cautions us. Our desire is to recognize God, to believe more deeply that this God, who shapes and abides in all creation, can be and is available to us (see *CCC*, #1, 27, 29, 35, 44).

God is involved and interested in our lives, in our history (see *CCC*, #32–35). The *General Directory for Catechesis (GDC)* tells us that theological reflection is based on the belief that God acts, always and everywhere, in human life (see *GDC*, #36–37). A friend has a plaque hanging in her office that reads, "Beckoned or not, God is here." That is the truth we seek to uncover and savor.

The Potential for Transformation

Often God is experienced "in our peripheral vision." Most of us do not have "thunderbolt" encounters with God. Theological reflection allows us to recall and savor the fleeting glimpses of God at work in our world and in our lives. It enables us to recognize the graciousness of God in life and allows us to root that belief in a felt experience. Information about or from the Christian tradition alone does not transform human experience. Engaging that tradition in a way that highlights the correlation between our faith heritage and our daily life, however, releases the potential for transformation (see *GDC*, #71). So as we bring forth our experience for reflection, we are engaging in a profound act of faith. We are trusting that the God of Israel, the Lord of restless, lost hearts, the God who journeys with us, the saving God of history, is with us and within us, involved in our current history and interested in our salvation (see *CCC*, #54–64). When we examine and attempt to clarify the actions and motivations of our lives, we can expect to see not just ourselves but signs and hints of God (see *CCC*, #99).

The prayer of one who engages in theological reflection is: "Lord, that I may see." As my family began grace before meals, my dad would always say, "Let us remember that we are in the holy presence of God." The De LaSalle Christian Brothers had taught him this—and it is the truth. We are always in God's presence, and sometimes we notice it. Theological reflection is the attempt to notice that truth more often. "Lord, that I might see." Once you begin to notice, you will see more—and the more you see, the more you'll see. That is the paradox. That is the truth. Anything can reveal the holy if we but see.

To engage in a theological reflection process is to see beneath the external elements of our life experience to the "God-touched" reality. It permits us, in some way, to encounter the "really real" beneath the "merely real." This God is not limited to one type of reality. Rather, God, who is infused in all creation, can be encountered in infinite ways, not merely the explicitly religious. How often have sunsets, concerts, children playing in a sand pile, or couples walking hand in hand been windows that give us a glimpse of God? "Lord, that I might see."

For Reflection

1. Think back to your years growing up. What did it mean "to be holy"? Who was or could be "holy"? How did you know if you were "holy" or "good"? What does holiness "look like" for you at this point in your life? What created the changes?

2. Try this exercise for a month and see what happens.

In the morning pray:

> Loving God, help me to see you in the people and events that touch my life today.

In the evening, let the people and events of your day pass before you and ask yourself:

> Where did I see God today? Where did I miss seeing God today?

CHAPTER 2

Theological Reflection: The Model

Gathering the Gear

The model of theological reflection I will share with you is often called the Whitehead Model. It is an adaptation of the model presented by Doctors James and Evelyn Whitehead in their book *Method in Ministry*. Their hope is to make accessible the process of theological reflection, to entice ministers to the wealth and value of engaging in it, and to help ministers facilitate that process with others.

The model presents to us three sources of religiously significant information to use in theological reflection.

- Experience (E)

- Tradition (T)

- Culture (C)

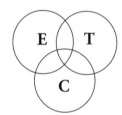

Experience

Experience is both simple and complex, encompassing the whole person—our ideas, feelings, insights, biases, and prejudices. Our Experience is simple in that it happens right now, right here. Our Experience is complex in that what happened to us in the past acts as a filter for our present Experiences. Experiences are complex in that some of them are run of the mill, others are planned, and still others come rushing in on us. Some we have control over; others are out of our control. Some we can handle, and others overcome us. Our Experiences are life!

Experience is more than ideas. In fact, for quality theological reflection to happen, our Experiences must carry some strong feelings so that we can engage in this dynamic process. We connect with others by sharing our Experiences with them. For although we are unique in all the world, we share similar feelings, hopes, and concerns. Thomas Groome, in *Christian Religious Education*, considers Experience as the present of things present, the present of things past, and the present of things future. Even in the "now," we are highly influenced by the past and the hopes and fears of the future. Who we are today is where we came from, and that influences how we are shaping the future.

Theological reflection that engages our Experience believes in the importance of God's continuing presence and action in human life. It is based on the belief that God acts always and everywhere in human life. Human experience is not transformed by information about or from the Tradition but rather by dialogue and interaction with the Tradition (see *CCC*, #94). In the dialogue we note the congruence and the challenges that each— Experience, Tradition, and Culture—brings to the interaction. It is in the dissonance and compatibility that the dynamic energy stimulates and moves us.

We may think that reflection on our personal experience is unique to today's time and culture. Some people say it's a product of a self-centered era and contend that earlier generations had neither the time nor the desire for reflection. As we look closely at our ancestors in faith, however, we find the story of a band of slaves who fled Egypt, wandered for years in the desert, and eventually found a home in a land called Israel. For some people these were experiences of escape, confusion, and survival. Others saw it differently; they perceived the protective and faithful presence of God in these events. They experienced Yahweh as their God and saw themselves as God's people. Thus the human experience of escape became a profound religious Experience for them.

Much later in their history, after the Northern Kingdom of Israel had fallen to the Assyrians and later the Southern Kingdom to the Babylonians, our ancestors in faith entered a soul-searching period in their lives. This period is often referred to as the Exile or the Babylonian captivity. During the Exile the Israelites felt that God was absent from their lives. As they were led into captivity by the Babylonians, they lost all their life anchors: their land, their beloved Jerusalem and holy Temple, their king, and their freedom. Yahweh, who had been present to them at the crossing of the Red Sea, seemed to abandon them as they crossed from the freedom of

Judah to the captivity of Babylon. They again had to reach deep inside themselves to bring forth what was written in the marrow of their bones. It was during this Exile that the Israelites began to see that it was the wisdom of God who had woven her way into and out of their lives, in the faithful and unfaithful times.

> *For she [Lady Wisdom] is a breath of the power of God,*
> *and a pure emanation of the glory of the Almighty;*
> *therefore nothing defiled gains entrance into her.*
> *For she is a reflection of eternal light,*
> *a spotless mirror of the working of God,*
> *and an image of his goodness.*
> *Although she is but one, she can do all things,*
> *and while remaining in herself, she renews all things;*
> *in every generation she passes into holy souls*
> *and makes them friends of God, and prophets.*
>
> (Wisdom 7:25–27)

When the Israelites thought they had lost everything, they discovered that the only thing that would sustain them was their faith in God. Adversity has a way of stripping away all that is not essential. The Israelites looked at all that had happened to them throughout history and, in looking more deeply, they began to see more clearly (see *CCC*, #54–64).

For Israel's descendants these events during the Exile continue to hold special significance reveal God's presence and purpose in human life. The Judeo-Christian Tradition can be seen as a constellation of human experiences that have been recognized as revealing God's presence and care for the world. Thus our ancestors in faith engaged in theological reflection on their Experience, calling upon their Tradition to relate to that Experience. They had an Experience of seeing deeply into life and finding God there. The more you see, the more you'll see. "Lord, that I may see."

In the musical *Joseph and the Amazing Technicolor Dreamcoat*, one of the songs contains the line, "I close my eyes, draw back the curtain, to see for certain what I thought I knew." Closing our eyes and drawing back the curtain is an apt metaphor for engaging in theological reflection. Drawing back the curtain so that we see more clearly the wonder of what is beyond the window is the "what" that theological reflection is all about. It is taking the Experiences of our lives and looking at them with new eyes—the eyes of one who wants to see more clearly, the eyes of one who wants to see life more deeply, the eyes of one who wants to see the wonders our God has done and is doing in our lives.

Tradition

Tradition includes sacred Scripture, the history of the Christian Church, and the teachings of our faith. It is important to recognize the pluriformity of the Tradition, which is one of the riches of our heritage. People often speak of the Tradition as a stagnant thing, but I have heard it said that "Tradition, our faith heritage, is the living faith of the dead, not the dead faith of the living." By exploring our Tradition through the process of theological reflection, we bring to life the treasure of faith.

We inherit a wealth of riches from our ancestors in faith. We lean on them. Distinguished theologian, scholar, and author Elizabeth A. Johnson gives a new and rich look at the understanding that we call the "communion of saints." In her book *Friends of God and Prophets*, she says, "For the symbol [communion of saints], somewhat abstract in itself, comes to birth in a river of holy lives through the centuries, a great crowd to which those confessing the creed today also belong, to which generations yet unborn and destined, and to which the natural world forms both matrix and partner" (p. 8).

We have this rich faith to draw upon. We have the power of the Spirit to call upon those who once lived, struggled, cried, and laughed over life to be present to us in this time and in this place.

We enjoy the fruits of a time-tested Tradition and, as we do theological reflection, we can bring that wealth into the conversation with our Experience and our Culture. When we engage in theological reflection, we so remember our past that it gives meaning to our present and direction for our future. Thus our faith can and does have meaning in our everyday life.

Not unlike our desire to search through our family tree and our family treasures, we seek to use the wisdom and the gifts that have been passed on to us. We want to garner the values, beliefs, and "tried-and-true" tenets of our faith. We pray ancient prayers that are meaningful and connect us to a long line of faithful believers. We study the Scriptures handed down through generations and ask how they speak to our lives today. How do the stories of Jesus challenge us at this moment in history? How does our Baptism impact our business transactions? our family life? our social relationships? Does the communion of saints bring insight to how we are raising our children?

We can "befriend the Tradition." That image softens the often distant feeling we sometimes get when speaking of the Tradition. Befriending the Tradition allows us to come close to—to become more familiar with—the Scriptures and the teachings of the Church. Theological reflection invites us to befriend the Tradition by letting it shed light on the experiences of everyday life. It pulls the Tradition forward and brings it to bear on life today. It garners the wisdom of living faith.

Conversely, we are formed by the very Tradition that we study and profess. The process of theological reflection offers opportunities to deepen understanding of our faith as well as to see the correlation between our faith and our daily life (see *GDC*, #147). A facilitator assists a group in dealing with areas of misunderstanding or lack of understanding. Chapter 5 explores the responsibility of the facilitator and suggests resources available to help in understanding the Tradition in its fullness.

Culture

As we become more aware of our personal feelings and convictions, as well as the Experiences that formed these feelings and convictions, we can begin to put them into dialogue with the

Tradition and *Culture*. Culture is so much a part of us that, unless circumstances take us out of the environment that supports our culture, we are hardly aware of it. Because we tend to assume its symbols, values, mores, and philosophies so naturally, we feel uncomfortable when we experience a clash in those underlying constructs of culture.

I recall my first year of teaching in Chicago. I was raised in the South, where "yes, ma'am" and "no, sir" were the appropriate responses to any question from an adult. Consequently, the first time a fourth-grade student answered me with a "yep," I was taken aback. I put my hand on my hip and said sternly, "What?" I could tell from the expression on the child's face that he had no idea what was upsetting me. In that brief encounter I realized the cultures of the South and the Midwest had just met and clashed! What would be considered rude in my hometown was absolutely appropriate in Chicago.

We actually belong to many cultures. For example, we come from a variety of nationalities: African American, Mexican, Irish, Vietnamese, Italian, Polish, and others. At the same time, we are Girl Scouts, cheerleaders, Knights of Columbus, catechists, ministers of the Eucharist, sisters, accountants, laborers, and priests. Each diocese and parish also has its own culture—"the way things are done around here." Each of the cultures to which we belong influences us. At times the values of one culture clash with the values of another, and we feel discomfort. When the values of one culture reinforce those of another, we feel supported.

In the process of theological reflection, if we position the messages and values of the Culture next to the Christian Tradition and our Experience, we notice both the clashes and the areas of support. Often we feel empowered by reflection to take action. Once energized by the insight gained by reflection, we can take that action.

FOR REFLECTION

1. *Experience*

Recall an event from the past week that has some meaning for you. Tell or write the story with as much detail and feeling as possible.

2. *Tradition*

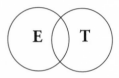

What Scripture story or religious teachings would shed light on that experience?

3. *Culture*

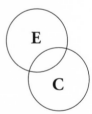

What would today's society say to you about the experience?

4. *Looking for the place of intersection*

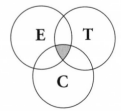

Looking at the three sources, or pieces—Experience, Tradition, and Culture—what have you learned from this exercise? What bit of wisdom have you learned from the experience?

The exercise started with Experience and moved to the Tradition. You searched the Tradition for stories or doctrines that would shed some light on your Experience. Then you considered the society or Culture in which you are living to see what it would say about your Experience. As you look at each piece of the model, you begin to move them together and give notice to the place where they intersect with one another. This is called putting the three into dialogue with one another. You are looking at your lived experience and using that Experience overlaid with Tradition and Culture to see the possibilities of meaning. Rather than considering each aspect independently of the other pieces, you deliberately let them enlighten, enhance, judge, and critique one another. It is the intersection of the model's three pieces on which theological reflection focuses.

CHAPTER 3

Theological Reflection: The Method

ΙΧΘΥΣ

Grab Your Fins, Face Mask, and Air Hose—and Dive Right In!

Experience, Tradition, and Culture are what we call the pieces, or "poles" of the model. The question is What do we do with them? We've got all the pieces, what's next? That's the method. The Whiteheads describe a three-step method:

- Attending

- Asserting

- Decision making

Attending

"Attending" is the skill of listening, giving ear to the wisdom and insights that each "pole" provides. The attending stage invites all the concerns, values, and information of a person's Experience, the Culture, and the Christian Tradition into a conversation, a dialogue. It is a time to explore hidden assumptions, hopes, and convictions, seeking information that is available in the Experience, Culture, and Tradition. This stage of the process requires certain skills.

First, we need to be alert to the movements of mind and heart within. We need to be honest about our prejudices, assumptions, reactions, areas of resistance, and motives in the conversation.

Second, on the interpersonal level, we need to be open to the experience of others. We must be able to withhold judgment so as to listen deeply to the values, convictions, biases, struggles, and hopes of the other. We need to suspend premature judgment and evaluation. In *The Art of Theological Reflection*, Killen and de Beer remind us that theological reflection calls us to transformation, not to certitude. If we are rigidly convinced of a single interpretation, we are not able to hear something new or unexpected and thus not able to engage in critical attending. We may not be able to receive new information and insights that challenge the way we see things. We may not be open to change. If we are to engage in meaningful theological reflection, however, we must let go of the need to be right.

We use the skill of attending to influence and be influenced by the Experience, the Tradition, or the Culture. The purpose of theological reflection is to move us from insight to action. By attending, we note shifts in our assumptions or convictions that allow us to rearrange our worldview. With a change or shift in worldview, a change in our actions often occurs. Such actions flow from a deeper, more reflective heart. We may not change a particular action, but we may have a clearer sense of the "why" behind it (see *GDC*, #53–56).

Attending is the first step in noticing the clashes and congruence of the dialogue partners. Attending is how we perceive things. We may use our five senses to see what is real, consider the facts, grasp the present situation, proceed step-by-step, and use skills with which we gather information. We may also attend by using our "sixth sense" to explore and consider future possibilities, learn new skills, and draw new insights. Attending invites us to look, to pay attention, to see. Attending is the Gospel call of Jesus to pay attention, to stay awake, to be alert. The psalmist cries out:

> They have mouths, but they do not speak;
> they have eyes, but they do not see;
> they have ears, but they do not hear,
> and there is no breath in their mouths.
>
> (Psalm 135:16–17)

This is a call to pay attention, to see with the eyes of the physical body and the eyes of the heart. It is a call to hear with the ears of the physical body but also with the ears of the heart. It is a call to attend to what is happening.

Asserting

"Asserting" is the second step in the method of theological reflection. This step flows naturally from receiving the information from the three poles of the model. Asserting engages the information from the three sources in a process of mutual clarification to expand and deepen religious insight. In this stage we ask: What does the Christian Tradition have to say about this? What messages would the Culture give to this situation? What have I learned from my Experience that will shed light on this question?

In the process of asserting we claim what we believe to be true. We may also come to a point where we deny a particular truth we have held yet at the same time lack the words to articulate a new truth. At the beginning of the Book of Job, for example, we find Job as a man who has everything a person could possibly want. Then we read that he has lost everything: possessions, relationships, and physical health. The Tradition (as well as Job) held that such calamities were punishments for either personal or ancestral sin, yet Job declared that he had not sinned.

This truth from his Experience challenges the truth held by the Tradition, even though Job did not have words to articulate a new truth. By the end of the book, we see a man who does not know why these calamities have happened to him, but he does know that they are not punishment for his sins or the sins of his ancestors. In other words, like Job, we can arrive at a point in our theological reflection where we can assert what we no longer hold to be true, even as we shift from one truth to a new truth. Sometimes it occurs on a personal level; other times it indicates a shift in the thinking of a larger community. Today this is often called a paradigm shift.

What happens to you when something you have held to be true for a long time no longer holds true for you? It can be a liberating process, but it can also be a painful process, involving the tension of letting go and holding on. What do you let go of? What do you hold on to? Can you let go when you don't yet have anything to grab onto? This is the "diving in and learning how to breathe differently" aspect of theological reflection. We are searching for a deeper truth that may be completely new or for a deeper understanding of a truth we have held. Moving through this process helps us grow in wisdom, truth, and understanding (see *GDC*, #56).

Think of asserting as a style of behavior that acknowledges the value of our own needs and convictions in a manner that respects the needs and convictions of others. In using the step of asserting, we avoid aggressive behaviors that limit us and prevent us from being open to transformation. We can be so cemented in a particular interpretation of the Christian Tradition, for example, that we are not aware of our own Experience or the wisdom of Cultural or other religious insights. We can be so blind that we close ourselves off to another's view. The "other" might be the Tradition, the Culture, or the other's Experience or view. Such aggressive behavior is destructive to the process of theological reflection because it can cut off any dialogue or exploration. It aborts reflection. To enter into theological reflection, we must be willing to suspend—for a while—what we hold to be certain.

When engaging in theological reflection, any of the three poles of the model can become the aggressor. When there is no room for dialogue with the Christian Tradition, we use the term *fundamentalism*. When only our own Experience has validity, we use the term *narcissism*. When only the Culture has the final and ultimate say, we use the term *secularism*. True theological reflection requires the truth and wisdom of each pole and the discipline to suspend judgment until all three have a hearing—a deeply interactive hearing. The ability to face diversity and tolerate ambiguity is a requirement of theological reflection. We must give up the need to be right. This letting go is, in itself, a process of transformation. We must be able to sustain different and possibly conflicting testimonies and realize that this ability is valuable and necessary to the process of theological reflection.

Decision Making

"Decision making" is the goal of theological reflection. The questions that move us to this point are: So what difference does this all make? What do we do with the insights gained from the assertive interaction of Tradition, Experience, and Culture? Where does this reflection lead? Was there an inner response, or does it require an outward movement? What is the cost of living an integrated life, one that blends and binds together the deepest values of our faith? What do we hope to gain by engaging in this process?" (see *Code of Canon Law*, #773).

John Shea suggests that the purpose of theological reflection in ministry is "to allow faith perspectives to influence personal and social life." We can gain clarity, set direction, choose action, and witness to our faith integrating with our life. Theological reflection is the process of bringing my inner world and my outer world into harmony. It is building congruence between my beliefs and my actions. It is "walking the talk" (see *CCC*, #849–851).

Toward the point of closure when facilitating a theological reflection group, I often ask: "So what. . . ? What difference will this experience, these insights, make in your life?" Or I invite a written response to these questions that begins, "Therefore, . . ."

Theological reflection calls us to transformation, and decision making is the moment in the process when we choose to respond to that call. It is the time when we find the insight and momentum to move faith into action. The theological reflection process of attending, asserting, and decision making, ". . . invites us to befriend our Christian heritage, our lived experience, our culture, and our contemporary faith community as conversation partners on the journey of faith" (Killen and de Beer, p. 3).

FOR REFLECTION

Recall an attitude, a belief, or a way of thinking that has changed for you.

1. How did this change come about?

2. What influenced this change?

3. How has this change made you different?

CHAPTER 4

Theological Reflection: How to Begin

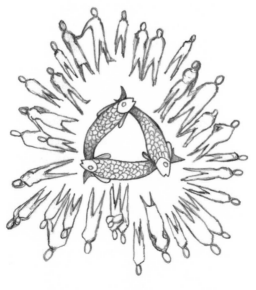

We're in the Water,
Now What?

We have a model with three poles: Experience, Tradition, and Culture. We have a method: attending, asserting, and decision making. Where do we go from here? Where do we begin?

Anything and anyone can be an occasion of reflection. That does not narrow the options much. We can begin theological reflection from any focus. A Scripture story, an event that has made an impression on us, a headline in the newspaper, or an occasion of clashing cultures: Any of these might create the need or desire for reflection. One of the wonders of theological reflection is that it can originate from many points of meaning and lead to deep reflection. Let's look at some examples.

Rite of Christian Initiation of Adults

"Breaking open the Word" is a familiar phrase to persons involved with the Rite of Christian Initiation of Adults (RCIA). Breaking open the Word begins with the Sunday Scripture readings and flows into personal reflection on the values, wisdom, and insights of the Word of God on the lives of the participants in today's world. When I was coordinator for the RCIA in a parish, one sponsor objected to the term "breaking open the Word." To him that was violent language. For me it parallels "breaking of the Bread," for as we are nourished by the Bread of Life, so too are we nourished by the Word of God. We break bread, eat, digest, and become bread for others. We break open the Word, digest it, and become the living Word for others. We enflesh the Word today in our very living. We become the Word made flesh. We take seriously the Incarnation. We become revelation.

That is the goal, but what is the process that makes it happen? What is the point of entry? In my role as a catechist, I reflect on the Sunday Scripture readings and listen for how they touch my life. Only then can I formulate questions that connect the readings to what is happening in the broader world or in daily life.

If the reading is about the good Samaritan, for example, I may ask, "Which people do you know who have gone out of their way in service to others?" Or I could ask, "Looking back over the week, can you recall an incident in which help came from an unexpected place?" (This is the step of attending to Experience.) I might invite the group to recall a story from the news that is good news. (This is an example of attending to Culture.) I allow time for silent reflection on those questions, and then I read aloud Sunday's Gospel, in this case, the story of the good Samaritan. (This is an example of attending to the Tradition.) After the reading, I pose a question that focuses the discussion and brings about reflection on the connection between the Gospel and the group members' personal Experience of goodness in their lives. (This is an example of putting the Tradition into dialogue with Experience and Culture; we are looking for the place of intersection.)

- Attending

- Asserting

- Decision making

Many people tell wonderful stories, and in their stories we see the good Samaritan walking the streets of Chicago, San Antonio, Boston, Miami, and Lexington. We find the good Samaritan in our families, among our colleagues, and in our neighborhoods. In reflecting together, we look at the good Samaritan in our own lives and are challenged by the call to be good Samaritans in our particular situations.

What about the step of decision making? That is the next step in the process. I often allow five to ten minutes for each person to write a reflection following these questions:

1. If you were to take this Gospel story of the good Samaritan to heart, what would you feel called to do?

2. If you were to live the values and message of this Scripture story, what one thing would you do this week to be a good Samaritan?

3. What would that "cost" you?

This is the "So what?" or "Therefore. . . ," the decision-making part of the reflection. It allows the insights gained from the dialogue to become more concrete in the lives of the participants. It invites a flow from discussion to action.

Finally, I invite the participants to share with one other person their intention or commitment for the week. Again, this allows the experience to deepen.

Maureen, a young woman in the group, gives us a good example. One evening the reading was the story of the widow's mite. Maureen said that she had been standing on a busy, downtown Chicago street corner on a cold, snowy day collecting money for a charity. Many people rushed by, bundled up and intent on moving swiftly; they hardly saw her in their attempts to brace themselves against the howling, frigid wind. One woman, however, wearing a tattered coat and frayed mittens, stopped to talk to Maureen. The woman wanted to know the cause she was collecting for. Maureen told her that it was for programs for children with mental retardation. The woman then pulled a dollar bill from her heavy sock and put it in the can. Maureen suspected it was her only dollar. She said she wanted to run after the woman and give her all the money in the container. She said she could not get that woman out of her mind.

That story shared within the group became the story of the group. That story carried a haunting sense of clarity about living this Gospel. After the discussion we reflected on the call of this Gospel in our individual lives, the questions being: If I were to take this Gospel to heart, what would it 'cost' me? What would be different in my life? What is being asked of me at this moment in my life? After taking time to write down their responses, the group members shared their commitments to live the Gospel in the context of their life situations. It was an opportunity for deeper sharing, accountability, and support.

Faith-Sharing Group

I ask individuals who gather in faith-sharing groups to reflect on a recent experience that carries a great deal of feeling. The event does not need to be dramatic, but it should hold meaning for them. After they narrate their stories I invite the group to name the important moments or shifts that took place in each story, and I list them on newsprint or a chalkboard. We then look at the elements gathered and try to find any similar story or similar elements in the Tradition. I invite the group to reflect on events in our world that may be reflected in this story. One question might be: What would people of our culture say about the story?

One woman shared that her husband had been unemployed for eight months. At first family and friends rallied around to encourage and support them. After awhile, however, people stopped calling or visiting because they didn't know what to say to the couple. Others "forgot" about them. Her frustrated husband vacillated between anger and debilitating depression. She never knew what mood he would be in. Her children became irritable.

The first response from the group was empathy and compassion for this woman. We understood her frustration and feelings of isolation and powerlessness. Once she felt a connection with the group members, it was tempting to stop there. Because we wanted to do a theological reflection process, however, we began with attending to the other two poles: Culture and Tradition.

We looked at the subtle messages of Culture: "Pull yourself up by your bootstraps." "A man is supposed to support his family." "Any job is better than no job." "We've carried you long enough; snap out of it." "Anyone who wants to work can find a job. After all, this is America, the land of opportunity." As we listed these cultural messages, we realized that we carried some of them within ourselves. Even when we knew they carried little truth, we found that they were deeply imbedded within our unconscious selves and influenced our biases.

We next looked at the Tradition and recalled the Gospel story of the laborers in the field. In the story those who arrived at the end of the day received the same wages as those who began at dawn. We remembered that the Spirit is said to fall upon the just and the unjust. The Spirit doesn't bless the working people more than those who are unemployed.

We also noted how abandoned Jesus felt in the garden of Gethsemane and as he hung on the cross. Judas, his friend and disciple, betrayed him with a sign of intimacy—a kiss. We know that Jesus invites everyone to come to him, especially those who hide in the shadows, or those on the fringes of life, like Zaccheus, the hunched-over woman, and the children who were pushed aside by the disciples. Jesus rearranges the criteria with regard to who will be first and who will be last. Worth does not come from wealth in Jesus' world. These values were listed on the board alongside the messages from the Culture.

Next we began to notice the clashes between the Experience of the woman telling the story, the messages and climate of the Culture, and the meaning of the Tradition. This woman's story became the Experience of the group, for we all have felt abandoned, caught in the middle, and scared. We have been molded by the Culture and carry within us the subtle messages of the society. We noted circumstances in which the Culture and Tradition offered support and comfort. We felt challenged by the woman's story and other stories of our faith Tradition and became more aware of our prejudices and biases. We were moved to examine our hearts and our actions and to compare them with the message and meaning of our deepest truth, our faith (see *GDC*, #26).

Transformation can happen for the whole group, not only for those who bring forth their experiences for reflection. Theological reflection can be an activity of deepening conversion. We enter the process both to influence and be influenced. Perhaps the shift that happens with and for us is confirming; it can also be confrontive. The process transforms us so that everyday life has increased depth. It is a process that brings our faith to life and life to our faith.

I have used the theological reflection process with seminarians. These young men had returned from spending several weeks in parishes doing pastoral ministry. During their time in the parish they were asked to write three verbatims, or "diaries," to use for theological reflection when they returned to the seminary. The verbatims gave participants in the theological reflection group written reports of pastoral encounters between the seminarians and the parishioners. One young man, for example, wrote the dialogue that occurred between him and a patient in a hospital or nursing home. Because the verbatim was the entry point for theological reflection, we began with the pole of Experience.

Al had just returned from a large parish with a long list of people whose illness kept them at home. It was the practice of the parish to have a minister bring Communion to these people on the first Friday of each month. Al set out with a list of thirteen parishioners to visit. By the end of the day, he was tired and felt less than enthusiastic. He felt as if he were was just "getting them all in." As he drove to visit Louise, last on the list, he remembered his assignment from the seminary and decided he'd better make this visit to Louise "count."

Louise was a widow who had become visually impaired. Although she had experienced many losses—her large home, her eyesight, her mobility, her frequent contact with friends and family, and the death of her husband—Louise was most gracious. At first Al thought it was a bit much, but as he listened to her he began to realize that this woman was grateful for all that God had given her and appreciated all that she had at the moment. He was aware mainly of her limitations, yet she was delighted with her gifts.

Each person in the theological reflection group read Al's report. Before the group began to discuss it, I asked Al how he felt about his verbatim now several weeks after the experience. He talked about his feelings for Louise, saying that she was an incredible person, and that her disposition was infectious. He admitted to feeling uplifted after visiting her, despite the grueling day he'd had.

The group discussed the various messages from the Culture about elderly persons, the unsighted, and those who have suffered great loss. Al knew his shock at Louise's attitude was based in his cultural assumptions about what makes a worthwhile life. We also explored the Tradition for insights into Al's Experience. What surfaced in the discussion were the healing stories of Jesus, reminders from St. Paul of the gifts given to us, the Transfiguration experience, and the spiritual and corporal works of mercy. When a group member mentioned the story of Veronica's veil, it seemed especially meaningful. Al had intended to bring Louise something: to offer a listening ear, a compassionate heart, and the Eucharist. He did offer that, indeed, but she also gave much to him. Just as Veronica offered the veil to wipe the face of Jesus on his way to Calvary, so did Jesus give Veronica the gift of his face imprinted on her veil. Al thought that he was the one bringing the gift; he was not prepared for the gift he would receive in return. The gift of this woman, in a very real sense, helped him see the face of Jesus.

"So what's happening out there?" Sometimes the doorway we enter is Culture. The events in our neighborhood, city, country, and world have an impact on us. One such event can be as simple as a change of seasons. The beginning of autumn can bring us to reflection on loss. The change of seasons can bring to mind the paschal mystery: the cycle of life, death, and new life. The leaves turn brilliant colors, cling to the branches, and finally surrender to the earth. The trees appear dead, but we know that spring will bring new life. The darkness of winter will be transformed by the light and color of spring.

We have autumn, winter, spring, and summer moments in our lives. We find stories in Scripture of the cycles of death and loss, redemption and resurrection. This is the cycle of life. It is the promise of our faith. Even when life appears finished, when death has its way, it is not the last word. The world beyond our Experience confirms the deep message of our faith Tradition. Reflection can allow us to see more deeply into the everydayness of life. "The whole Earth is full of [God's] glory" (Isaiah 6:3), and sometimes we notice. The more you see, the more you'll see. "Lord, that I might see."

My religious congregation recently helped build a house with Habitat for Humanity on property belonging to the community. We used this Experience to reflect on building a house for others and on the building of the reign of God. We started with the tangible aspects—the hammer, nails, dream, and grunt work—of planning the project: calling the community of laborers, building the foundation and framework, and dealing with the conditions of land and weather.

Next we looked at Culture: working without wages; giving time and labor to people we did not know; emphasizing that everyone do a piece of the project instead of relying on experts; and working side-by-side with people from all walks of life—judges, children, electricians, teachers, bankers, farmers, cooks, homemakers, and doctors. Through this experience, we knew in our bones the Experience of faith in action. Through shoulder-to-shoulder labor, we witnessed the depth of unity that can exist among persons of different cultures, lifestyles, and faith traditions. "Let us build the city of God" was more than a song. It was a project that connected people who had never met before, to provide a safe shelter for a family who participated in building their home alongside of "strangers." That structure gives witness to a Gospel that has a heartbeat. Everyone who participated in any way can pass by that house and remember the joy and strain of building—together—the city of God.

Religious Education Class

Often in our religious education classes the starting point is a theme from the Tradition: the sacraments, the Commandments, the Incarnation, the paschal mystery, or Scripture. Although these topics can provide ready access to the theological reflection process, we can enter the process also through other doorways.

Let's consider the theme of reconciliation, for example. Begin by asking questions that can tap into the Experience of the class. The questions should be age-appropriate. I have found, however, that the simpler the questions are, the more engaged the rest of the group tends to be. Consider beginning with the following questions:

Recall a time when you hurt someone.

How did you feel? What did you do? Did you reconcile with this person?

Who initiated the reconciliation? How did you feel afterwards?

If there had been no reconciliation, how would you feel?

When did you feel you did not deserve forgiveness, but were granted it anyway?

When you hurt others, what do you do to make up with them?

Next, look at the Tradition with questions such as:

What does God tell us about reconciliation?

Which stories from Scripture involve forgiveness?

What does Jesus tell us about reconciliation: when we have been hurt, when we hurt another, when we break our relationship with God?

Why does the Church provide the Sacrament of Reconciliation?

What does that tell us about God?

Then look at Culture with questions such as:

What does our Culture say about forgiveness?

What do we see in our justice system that speaks to this issue?

How do these messages relate to the message of the Gospel?

All the poles have something to say, so let the dialogue begin!

As the class struggles with their Experience, the Tradition, and the Culture, insights will emerge on the meaning of the gift of reconciliation. The dialogue will highlight areas of congruence and areas of dissonance. Often the Tradition will challenge the assumptions of the Culture. Those insights will, in turn, challenge the Experience of the participants. As believers in the call to be reconciled and to be reconcilers, we participate in the Church's mission of reconciliation (see *GDC*, #21, 26). We are called to transformation: to be transformed and to help transform others (see *GDC*, #26).

At the conclusion of dialogical reflection, allow time for silence. I call this "steep and savor" time. Invite the group to write their personal insights and reflections, the "So what . . ." and "Therefore . . ." Questions they will want to reflect on include:

What concepts or understandings shifted for me?

What did I learn?

If I were to explain the gift of reconciliation to my younger brother or sister, how would I describe it?

Who do I need to forgive at this time?

From whom do I need forgiveness?

For Reflection

Look in your kitchen cabinet for a cup with a crack or chip. Just hold the cup for a while. In some ways it is "broken."

1. *Experience*

Recall a time in your life when you felt especially broken.

What were your feelings?

How did you or others describe you during this time?

How did others react?

What or who helped you to heal?

2. *Culture*

   Reflecting the Culture:

   What does society say should be done with things that are broken? Write these things down.

   Reshaping the Culture:

   In this day of "recycle and reuse," what are some other things you could do with the broken cup? Write them down.

3. *Tradition*

   Read Luke 13:10–16. This is the story of the hunched-over woman.

   What did the Culture of the day say should be done with this woman?

   What would be the normative behavior toward anyone who had a mental or physical deformity during this time?

   What does Jesus do in the story?

   What is Jesus saying in the story?

4. *Looking for the place of intersection*

   Looking at the three pieces—Experience, Tradition, and Culture—what have you learned from this exercise? What bit of wisdom have you learned from the experience? (Adapted from Killen and de Beer, *The Art of Theological Reflection*, p. 103.)

CHAPTER 5

Theological Reflection: The Facilitator

Keeping the Gear Untangled

Although we can do theological reflection alone, our purpose is to explore the process of theological reflection in groups (see *GDC*, #159). With that in mind, it is important to examine the elements of a group climate that welcome and promote a theological reflection process. We are attempting to develop a communal spirituality similar to that of Jesus and his community. A good size for a faith-sharing group is from eight to ten people. Doing theological reflection with a larger group, however, such as an RCIA group or a group of students, is certainly appropriate and possible.

Some groundwork is necessary to create an environment for a theological reflection group. The facilitator provides both the physical and interpersonal climate that welcomes and encourages faith sharing. It is important for the facilitator to be prepared and to know the goals, the purpose, and the direction of the group. Faith sharing requires reciprocity between the faith story and one's own story. It requires the sharing of one's own story with others and listening attentively and reverently to their stories. Group facilitation skills can provide an environment for such interaction to take place smoothly and with respect for all involved in the process.

You as the Facilitator

As facilitator your work is to encourage dialogue among the group members. You create a safe group environment by encouraging thoughtful listening and stressing that all sharing is confidential; what is shared in the group remains within the group. Allow many ideas and perspectives to surface without needing to resolve them. Invite and welcome differences. Diversity of opinion and life experience is a gift.

The following key items will help you facilitate a theological reflection group:

- Encourage all to use "I" messages rather than "You" messages. We take personal responsibility for our own opinions when we say, "I think or I feel. . . ." "I" messages allow people to maintain responsibility for their own thoughts and actions, instead of placing that power in the hands of another. So often we find ourselves inclined to say, "You make me so mad (or happy or irritable or pleased, and so on) when. . . ." Such statements make our own feelings conditional on another's actions or feelings. It may take time to move the group from making "You" statements to "I" statements, but it is time well spent.

- Let silence emerge in the group and hold it without becoming anxious. Silence promotes space for sacred stirrings within the group and within the individual members. If silence goes too long, you can say, "I'm not sure what the silence means." Then allow the group to respond and grapple together.

- Keep the group focused. There are times when the people speaking get lost in their own words or begin to ramble. When that happens, interrupt by saying, "I'm losing the point you are trying to make. Could you rephrase it in a sentence or two?" If humor or disruptive comments are taking over the conversation, call the focus back by saying, "We seem to have drifted, so let's pause for a moment and attend to the question at hand."

- Avoid generalizations or platitudes. To keep comments specific, ask, "What does that mean for you?" rather than "What does that mean?"

- Keep the discussion open. Remind yourself and the group to suspend judgment and certitude.

- Summarize. Periodically take time to summarize what has been said by asking, "Where are we at this point?"

The tendency in the group might be to address the facilitator. When this happens, consider looking at other members of the group rather than at the speaker who is addressing you. You need not reply to each comment made by a group member; let someone else in the group comment. If necessary, ask the group, "Are there any reactions to that?" Listen deeply to others, and listen to what you are hearing. As facilitator, avoid being the first person to respond to the person who has spoken.

Gaining Clarity About Feelings

People often are unaware of how they feel or what their deepest issues are. As facilitator you (or a member of the group) do not help by "solving" the concern for another person. Real helping often means encouraging others to express themselves in order to come to clarity about their feelings or concerns.

Often the best strategy is to stand by as people struggle to articulate themselves or listen to themselves. Some typical ways of assisting or being with others as they attempt to come to clarity are:

- Listening deeply, especially to feelings

- Clarifying anything you don't understand

- Saying, "Can you give us an example of _____?"
    "Could you tell us more about this?"
    "I'm not sure I understand what you mean by
    _____."
    "Are you saying _____?"

- Acknowledging the feelings that you hear

- Checking out what you think you understand

The following chart lists the various types of listening and their purposes. It also gives examples of listening.

Types of Interactive Listening

TYPES	PURPOSE	EXAMPLES
1. Clarifying	To get additional facts To help explore all sides of an issue	"Can you clarify this?" "Do you mean. . . ?" "Is this your concern as you see it now?"
2. Restatement	To check out meaning and interpretation with the other To show you are listening and you understand what the other is saying	"As I understand it, your point is . . ." "This is what you have decided to do because . . ." "You feel _____ because . . ."
3. Neutral	To convey that you are interested and that you are listening To encourage the person to continue talking	"I see." "Uh-huh." "That's very interesting." "Say more about _____."
4. Reflective	To show that you understand how others feel about what they are saying To help people reflect on their own feelings	"You feel that _____." "As you saw it, it was _____."
5. Summarizing	To bring all the discussion into focus in terms of a summary To serve as a springboard for further discussion on a new issue	"These are the key ideas you have expressed. . . ." "If I understand how you feel about the aspect or situation, . . ."

As leader or facilitator of a group, you need to remember that listening is an act of love. Because it seems at times to be passive, you may not realize that it is a profound gift. When you listen to another person, you use more than your ears! Listening requires that you open yourself to another person.

A desire to "fix things," give advice, or correct the problem often gets in the way of deep listening. Persons who confide in you or in members of a group usually don't want advice; they want someone to hear, to understand, and to care about what is happening. Help others in the group recognize the gift of deep listening and receiving the gift of another's sharing.

Staying with the Experience

The following checklist will help you stay with the experience that is being shared:

Do

- Listen with everything you have.

- Receive gratefully another's experience.

- Allow speakers to be responsible for their own feelings and life.

- Affirm speakers by relaying back the experience you hear.

- Ask speakers if they wish to say anything else. An open-ended question can make the sharing more complete: "How are you doing now?" or "How does this experience affect you now?"

- Allow for periods of silence during the session. They help.

- Help people stay with "I" statements and personal experience.

Don't

- React immediately or jump in with your experience.

- Give advice or try to problem solve.

- Try to change another or make everything better.

- Try to take away or explain away feelings.

- Add your interpretation.

- Pry for curiosity's sake.

- Fill every moment with talk.

- Allow generalizations like "we," "they," or "people."

Guidelines for Faith Sharing

The purpose of the theological reflection group is faith sharing, connecting life with faith. There is a distinction between the sharing in this type of group and other groups. The guidelines for faith sharing must be clear to keep a clear focus for theological reflection groups:

Sharing is voluntary.

- No one is required to share.

- Verbal participation is encouraged but not demanded.

- The tone of the session is invitational.

Sharing is not interrupted.

- When someone is sharing, everyone listens before commenting or speaking.

- Side conversations are avoided.

- Only one person speaks at a time.

Sharing is not contradicted.

- The sharing is based on the person's own experience; therefore conclusions or critiques of what is shared are not appropriate.

- Avoid trying to take away feelings with comments like, "You shouldn't feel that way."

Sharing is done in "I" language.

- The sharing begins with "I think" or "I feel" rather than "Mary said" or "Joe thinks."

- Questions should elicit "I" language.

Sharing is confidential.

- Confidentiality is a key element if trust is to be built into the group.

- What is shared in the group stays in the group.

Furthermore, members need to understand the difference between dialogue and debate also needs to be noted. People often assume there is a "right" answer, and thus seek to find that correct answer or prove their point. This attitude does not work well in a faith-sharing group. Distinctions between debate and dialogue include:

DEBATE AND DIALOGUE

Debate

Dialogue

Assumes that there is a right answer, and that some people possess it

Assumes that many people have pieces of the truth and that together they can craft a new solution

Is combative: participants attempting to prove the other side wrong

Is collaborative: participants working together toward common understanding

Is about winning

Is about exploring common ground

Listens to find flaws and make counter-arguments

Listens to understand, finding meaning and agreement

Defends assumptions as truth

Reveals assumptions for re-evaluation and learning

Critiques the others' positions

Re-examines all positions

Defends one's own views against those of others

Admits that others' thinking can improve on one's own

Searches for flaws and weaknesses in others' positions

Searches for strength and value in others' positions

Seeks a conclusion or vote that ratifies one's own position

Seeks new options, not closure

Framing the Questions

Besides setting guidelines, creating a safe environment for faith sharing also involves framing the questions. How the questions are asked is very important. It is important that you spend time formulating good questions. The following list outlines steps that will help you prepare questions for dialogue in the theological reflection group. They will serve as a springboard for the sharing.

1. If you are beginning with the Scripture readings, pray over the Scripture before you create the questions or process. Use whatever background material is available in your preparation. Leave room and time for the Spirit to work within you.

2. Craft open-ended questions. Do not, for example, pose questions that will elicit "yes" or "no" answers or ones that suggest a predetermined answer. Help the group identify faith experiences without making a judgment about the morality of their experience.

3. Develop questions that help people recall personal experiences and then gradually draw them forth to see the manifestation of God in these life experiences.

4. Avoid religious jargon in the questions.

5. Keep questions simple.

6. Avoid words that make people feel that their experiences must be extraordinary to have worth. Don't ask things like: "Recall a time when you felt the most overwhelming presence of God in your life."

7. Provide time for quiet, personal reflection. After the Scripture reading, allow a moment of quiet to let the Word of God wash through and over the group.

8. When appropriate, focus the listening on the Word. If you are using, for example, the story of Jesus asking the blind man, "What do you want me to do for you?" (Luke 18:35–43) you might say to the group, "Take a moment to relax and recall that we are, as always, in God's presence." Then pause for a moment

and continue: "Tonight we will hear Jesus ask, 'What do you want me to do for you?' I invite you to think about what is happening in your life right now. If Jesus asked you, 'What do you want me to do for you?' what would be your response to him? Just spend a quiet moment within your own heart to respond to Jesus." Then after a moment, without any introduction, proceed to the reading.

9. Prepare more than one question for the reflection. If the first question does not seem to draw a response from the group, then put forth a new question. It is also appropriate to ask the group what the silence means. It might mean they need more time, or they might need a new question.

10. Develop good starters such as: "Recall a time when you . . ."; "Describe an experience from your own life when . . . "; "From your personal experience, think about . . ."

11. Poor starters include comments such as these: "Isn't it true that . . ." (predetermined answer);

"Don't you think . . ." (wonder if they don't think the same thing as you);

"Tell the group . . ." (authoritative, not invitational).

12. Sometimes it is helpful to divide the group into smaller groups of two or three, and ask people to share one-on-one. Doing so allows additional time for personal sharing and can help build a sense of closeness among the members.

13. Center large group sharing on the "So what . . ." (decision-making) part of the reflection. Allow time for members to write in their journals before sharing in the large group. Ask: "What new insights did you gain from the reflection and sharing? What surprised you? What challenged you? How will you apply these insights to your daily life?"

14. Encourage the group to stay with the question until the next meeting. When you gather again you might begin by asking: "What has happened since we were last together?" or "How did

the insights from our last meeting stay with you?" or "What came to mind since that time?"

Challenges and Gifts Within a Group

No matter the nature of the task, some persons in each group assist the flow of the process and others challenge it. Some persons are skilled at sharing and listening, and for others this is difficult. Those who struggle with understanding effective group interaction often become problems within the group. Here are some examples of such problems, found in any given group, and strategies to help you deal with them should they arise.

Talking about others: Sometimes you find persons who enjoy talking about others. The conversation can deteriorate into a gripe and gossip session. You may need to remind the group that it has come together to share faith and listen to the stories of the group. At times confronting gossip creates some tension, but most likely others also want the talk to stop but don't know how to stop it.

Monopolizers: Monopolizers are persons (facilitator or participants) who will not stop talking or interrupting. Keep in mind that people have come to this session to share with one another, not to listen to someone's lecture. Although the advantage of monopolizers is that they can get sharing started, the drawback is that they have a hard time stopping. You need to be firm with monopolizers without being offensive. Monopolizers very often are unaware of their behavior, so talk privately to those who tend to be monopolizers—together you might even work out a signal you can use in the group. Monopolizers usually are not trying to manipulate the group; they are simply eager (perhaps overly so) to participate. Monopolizers may also be persons who are not comfortable with silence. When there are monopolizers in the group, group rules can be restated at the beginning of each session. One example might be to say, "Let's give everyone a chance to share before we take a second turn." Another approach might be to say, "There are some people who have not had a chance to share; let's allow them some space to do that."

Manipulators: These persons can be destructive to the group and to you as facilitator. They can use many forms of manipulation: silence, sarcasm, body language, side conversations, under-the-breath remarks, sighs, yawns, or monopolizing. You might have to confront them privately. At some points you might have to confront them in the group, if the group's health is at stake. Manipulators can poison the air for everyone.

The Scripture quote-giver or "God-talker": "God-talkers" love to give a Bible reference for everything. You have to gently lead them to speak from their life experience, connecting Scripture to their lived experience. It helps if you restate the purpose of the gathering right at the beginning to refocus on sharing life experience.

Conciliators: Conciliators are helpful; they enable people to be comfortable with differences of personality and opinions and reactions. They tend to create a spirit of tolerance within the group, and they show great respect for individuals.

Morale boosters: Morale boosters compliment, acknowledge, and encourage the contributions of each member. They tend to make people feel good about themselves and the contribution made. They may come across as Pollyanna, however, and may not recognize the complexities and real problems of life.

Elaborators: Elaborators clarify and expand their experiences with great detail. The positive aspect of their sharing is that they help the group (and themselves) to get the most out of their experiences. They can, however, drive the point into the ground well past the point at which the group already understands it. As facilitator you can interrupt the elaborator if the group is getting bored or exasperated. Simply asking the group if they understand the elaborator's point will confirm that all are on board, and allow the process to continue.

Synthesizers: Synthesizers are gifts in a group. They have the skill to take what has been expressed (verbally and nonverbally) and present it back to the group (synthesize it). "We seem to be saying . . . "; "It seems that the feelings around this issue are . . ." The group always has the responsibility for verifying the perceptions or observations of the synthesizer.

You can help the group learn helpful group skills by the way you facilitate the group. Making "I" statements and reminding others to do the same raises consciousness for the members of the group. By attending to each person, inviting reflective responses, using open-ended questions, and honoring silence in the group, you mentor the group in positive skills for its members.

For Reflection

1. Recall an experience of positive sharing in a group. What made it so? Which ground rules were honored? What skills did the facilitator use to promote healthy group life?

2. Recall an experience of negative sharing in a group. What made it so? Which ground rules were not honored? What could the facilitator have done? What could the group have done? What could you have done?

3. What skills do you provide that enhance the flow of a group?

4. Which patterns do you find difficult in a group discussion?

5. How might you encourage behavior that enhances a group discussion?

CHAPTER 6

Theological Reflection: The Discipline of Authenticity

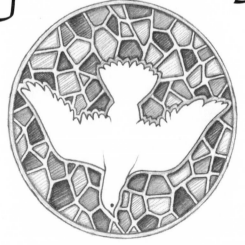

Anchors, Life Jackets, Moorings

◆

Just as groundwork is necessary to facilitate the interaction of the theological reflection groups, so is adequate preparation essential to establish the foundation for dialogue with the Tradition. Frequently, people believe the religious Tradition is what they remember from their early religious education. While that is an important component in our faith development, the Tradition we engage in theological reflection is the doctrines, dogmas, teachings, and understandings of sacred Scripture given to us by the Church. The Tradition is living, and the Church reflects upon and brings new light and insight to the tradition in every age.

Facilitators Serve as Formed and Informed Resources

The responsibility of facilitators of theological reflection groups is to attend to their own theological understanding to serve as formed and informed resources to the group. Facilitators carry out this responsibility through continuous study, both formal and informal, since study is basic to their role.

They provide the group with the "anchor" for theological understandings consistent with our faith Tradition. They also provide resources for the group as needed to keep the relationship—the interaction between Experience, Tradition, and Culture—focused and within the boundaries of the authentic teachings of the Church.

Many resources are available to support the work of facilitators in this task, and it is their responsibility to avail themselves of such resources.

Facilitators Are Deep Listeners

Attending to each pole—Experience, Tradition, and Culture—requires the discipline of listening intensely. It calls facilitators to put aside their biases and listen deeply. Patricia O'Connell Killen, in *Journeys in Ministry*, describes the responsibility of facilitators to "help others see the depth to which our life experiences resonate with Christian tradition and reveal God's activity in our midst" (p. 103). To accomplish that goal, facilitators must have a firm grasp of the Tradition and be able to recognize the signs of God's activity, which are often subtle and elusive.

Many of us listen for the connections of others' experiences to our own. The strength of that connection is the experience of communion and commonality. The liability in hearing our story in another's is making the other's story more ours than the property of the other person. Similarly, in listening deeply to Tradition, we hear the Church's wisdom that has been handed down to us, and that is what we bring to the dialogue—not simply our personal interpretation of the Tradition. We have been given a treasure (see *GDC*, #94–96); the role of facilitators and catechists is to bring that treasure and its richness to theological reflection.

Facilitators Are Faithful to the Tradition

Facilitators look for the theological themes engaged in the process. Fidelity to the Tradition requires an understanding of the doctrines and teachings of the Church. We bring to the conversation of theological reflection the Word of God as the Christian community has received it, understands it, celebrates it, lives it, and communicates it in many ways. This is fidelity to the Tradition (see *GDC*, #105–106).

People in theological reflection groups have their unique personal experiences. They have their unique interpretation of the cultural influences in their lives. Central to the process of theological reflection, however, is an understanding of the doctrines of our faith, which is true to the Tradition. The *CCC* notes the intimate connection between sacred Scripture and Tradition, yet it also recognizes the distinctions of each. Quoting the *Dogmatic Constitution on Divine Revelation (Dei verbum),* the *CCC* defines sacred Scripture as "the speech of God as it is put down in writing under the breath of the Holy Spirit" (#81). Holy Tradition constitutes the doctrines that have been handed down to us by the Church. Holy Tradition and Scripture are bound together because they have the same source and goal (see *CCC,* #78–82).

Attending to Preparation

Each of us is called to continuous study of the Tradition. We explore its meaning and how it applies to our life and the life of the Church. Doing so is the heart of our ongoing development in understanding the faith we profess. As facilitators of theological reflection groups, however, we must prepare ourselves for the groups we lead. Our preparation is necessary and critical for the well-being of the process and the members of the group. So how do we prepare? What are some specific ways we can attend to this responsibility?

The first task is to pay attention to the group. In chapter 4 we considered the kinds of groups and how to apply theological reflection to them. Let's now consider our theological preparation for each.

RCIA: Breaking open the Word is the model of theological reflection used in the RCIA process. Numerous resources are available to provide background and a firm theological foundation for the interaction. Breaking Open the Word of God: Resources for Using the Lectionary for Catechesis in the RCIA, the series edited by Karen Hinnan Powell and Joseph P. Sinwell, offers understandable and thorough development of the theological themes found in the Scripture readings for each Sunday. Three books, one for each lectionary cycle (A, B, and C).

Foundations in Faith, the series published by Resources for Christian Living, also offers a wealth of background and direction for each of the cycles.

As you develop themes in the RCIA, audiovisual material can assist you. Catholic Update videos by St. Anthony Messenger Press and Franciscan Communications offer some valuable tools, such as *Eucharist: Celebrating Christ Present* and *Understanding the Sacraments*. *The Great Mysteries: An Essential Catechism* by Andrew M. Greeley engages many central elements of our Tradition and is an excellent resource for theological reflection. These resources enable people to develop a deeper understanding of the elements of our faith Tradition and a language with which to engage in theological reflection.

Faith-Sharing Groups: The RCIA begins with the Scriptures in breaking open the Word, so I often use the Sunday readings as an entry into the theological reflection process with faith-sharing groups. In preparation for the sharing, I look to commentaries that will illuminate for me the meaning and message of the readings. Several sources include: The Catholic Study Bible: New American Bible and the Read and Pray series, edited by Robert J. Karris, O.F.M. The New Testament Reading Guide is a series of fourteen booklets that explores the books of the New Testament. The Liturgical Press offers the Collegeville Bible Commentary, which is a set of eleven booklets that also covers the New Testament books. Liturgy Training Publications provides numerous supportive materials, such as *Workbook for Lectors and Gospel Readers* and *Sourcebook for Sundays and Seasons*. *The New Jerome Biblical Commentary*, edited by Raymond E. Brown, SS, Joseph A. Fitzmeyer, SJ, and Roland E. Murphy, O Carm, provides a context and background for scriptural reflection and discussion.

When a group begins theological reflections from the standpoint of Culture or Experience, correlation with the Tradition may require having the members assist in suggesting theological themes. Facilitators who do not feel adequately steeped in understanding of certain themes might suggest that, between sessions, participants commit themselves to reflection on a particular theme and doing some research into the understanding of that doctrine, Scripture passage, and so on. Facilitators could then do their "homework" in preparation for the following session. Resources can be books, classes, teachers, or priests. Although this approach may feel awkward initially, how blessed are we to be motivated to explore the concerns of our faith. How meaningful this exploration can be.

In cases in which participants have little understanding of the Tradition, facilitators might need to take the initiative in suggesting themes that correlate with group members' Experience and Culture. Sometimes you may discover that the interpretation of the Tradition is not faithful to the teachings of the Church or the understanding of Scripture. Often people take a literal approach to understanding the Scriptures. This issue may require a separate session on how Catholics understand the Scriptures. If you, as facilitator, feel inadequate in providing that catechesis, bring in a resource person.

Another resource for understanding how to interpret the Scriptures is a video by Sandlestrap Technologies, Inc. titled *Introduction to Scripture*. It is part of the series Seeds of Faith, tape C. Articles that offer a deeper theological basis to themes that emerge in the group not only help participants develop a theological base that anchors the group; they also strengthen the participants' faith foundation. Catholic Update by St. Anthony Messenger Press offers reader-friendly and theologically sound presentations on multiple themes of our Tradition.

A further resource that provides an understanding of the significance of the Second Vatican Council is the video series, The Faithful Revolution. Published by Resources for Christian Living, this resource offers five sixty-minute videos with study guides. *While You Were Gone: A Handbook for Returning Catholics and Those Thinking About It*, by William J. Bausch, also treats theological themes in a reader-friendly fashion.

I encourage facilitators to become familiar with the resources available for their own theological development as well as for providing some grounding and creating the context for interaction with the Tradition.

Religious Education Class: Using theological reflection in religious education class most frequently begins with a theme from the Tradition. Manuals that accompany the student texts offer theological background and understanding that is age-appropriate and sensitive to the foundational beliefs of the Catholic Church. These manuals often suggest support resources, such as books, videos, and articles that can enhance the teacher's understanding of the particular theme presented. Again, it is important to use the resources available so that the Tradition we pass on is the Tradition of the Catholic Church, not merely the memory of how it was for us. Continuing to renew and develop our understanding of the components of our faith enriches our living of that faith as well as our gifting others with it.

FOR REFLECTION

1. What are the areas of theological understanding that you believe are your strong suits? For example, you may choose the Eucharist.

2. Read an article from *U.S. Catholic* (Claretian Publications) or Catholic Update (St. Anthony Messenger Press) about the Eucharist (or another area of theological understanding).

What did you learn from your reading?

What did you believe that was confirmed? What concept or belief was deepened?

What was challenged? How were you stretched? How did you feel about that?

How did what you learned affect your faith life? How will it affect your teaching and facilitating?

3. What current writings about the Eucharist could you search out?

4. What does the Church teach about sacraments today?

CHAPTER 7

Theological Reflection: What's It to Me?

Surfacing—and Then
"Walking on Water"

W e've looked at the model, the method, and the
dynamics of groups. We have the tools and we
have the process—so we're on our way. Before we
head off to plan our groups, however, let's take a look at the
what's-in-it-for-me aspect.

At the end of each session, I ask the "So what. . . ." or
"Therefore. . . ." question. Perhaps it's time for us to look at the
"So what. . . ." question as a facilitator. Besides all the preparation
and planning for the group, what about you? Is this just one more
idea you can add to your repertoire of offerings to a group? a new
project that might attract some new people? "Unless the Lord
builds the house, those who build it labor in vain" (Psalm 127:1).

One of the goals of the spiritual life is increased awareness of
the deeper dimensions of life. We say prayers so that we can
become pray-ers. We do to be. We practice dance steps and learn
all the movements so that we can become dancers. I once had a
professor who said that he ran each day in order to float. Because
I was not a runner and had little aspiration to be, I didn't have
any idea what he meant. Over the years that image comes back,
however, because I do know the discipline of doing, of acting, so
that I may be different. We practice disciplines so that we might
become spontaneous. We develop a strategy so that it becomes
natural, so that it becomes a way of life (see canon 773).

Theological reflection provides the framework for us to look
deeply into what could otherwise be missed or dismissed as just
an ordinary experience. We spend time doing the disciplines of
attending, asserting, and decision making so that we can be different in the world. Once we begin to see deeply, we begin to see
depth more frequently. When that happens, the world takes on a
new cast. The more you see, the more you'll see. The glimpses of
the sacred become more frequent because we have learned to see
differently. We take time away so that the time "not away" may
more readily be revelation to us. We learn to dive in and savor the

mystery that is our life. Then, in surfacing, we carry with us the treasure of that dynamic. The psalmist aptly suggests that we build in vain unless the Lord builds with us.

I am often asked to lead days of reflection for women. Sometimes the person making the request asks me to talk on Martha and Mary from the Gospels. So many people feel like Martha and think they should be more like Mary. They are convinced that one day spent in reflection will be just the booster shot that will transform all Marthas into Marys!

I always decline this kind of request and instead recommend something that will help people consider where the holy is in their lives. I suggest a title such as: "Who Me, Holy? Ya Gotta Be Kiddin'!" That grabs their attention and speaks to what people so often try to hide. We all think there is a holiness goal out there somewhere, and we know we fall short of it. When we can consider the spiritual in our lives as already there, albeit not noticed, we long to deepen it. The more you see, the more you'll see.

I ask: "So what does carpooling have to do with spirituality?" Or I suggest that contemplation is closely connected to the vigilant parent caring for a sick child or waiting up late for a teenager to come home. Once people make the connection between their ordinary lives and their spiritual lives, they can "walk on water." They've seen the depth and have learned to surface. They know how to dive deeply and have discovered how to live with the insights, challenges, and sensitivities that reflection can provide. They have learned to tap into the life-giving well that Jesus promised the Samaritan woman and promises us (see *CCC,* #2013, 2028). They have learned that anything can be revelation if we but see. "Lord, that I may see."

There was a plaque on the wall at a university where I once taught. It looked as if strips of wood had been glued onto a board at various angles. At first I thought it probably "spoke" to someone interested in contemporary art. After awhile, however, I actually "saw" it. Those pieces of wood "randomly" positioned and glued in place actually spelled Jesus. It was an optical illusion. Once I saw it, although I had always seen it, I wondered how I had missed it so often. Theological reflection allows us the opportunity to see revelation where it is, to see the divine veiled in the most and least obvious places in our lives. The more you see, the more you'll see.

Reciprocity: The Nature of Ministry

As pastoral ministers, we provide opportunities for others to learn our sacred Tradition, to celebrate our sacred rituals, and to experience divine activity in our lives. One of the blessings of ministry is that we, too, are gifted by the very gift we give. I know that I love to teach because I learn so much. I teach to learn as well as to give away what has so graciously been given to me. I prepare liturgies and prayer services for others, but the treasure for me is that I am brought to prayer in the very preparation.

Ministers of care always say that they get more than they give. This is the paradox of ministry: We are blessed as we offer blessing. As we give the gifts of our time, skill, knowledge, and presence, we too are given a sacred gift in return. We begin with a generous heart and assume that giving moves in one direction—out from us. What we discover, again and again, is that reciprocity is the nature of ministry—and it comes unexpectedly.

We give the gift of planning and facilitating to the groups we serve. The truth is that we work diligently to provide an atmosphere, guidelines, and a process to make the groups work well. We often discover, however, that we are enriched by the interaction and the privilege of seeing the divine unfold in the lives of the participants. We can find God in the most unexpected places. The God of surprise can continue to astonish us, and bring us to deeper faith. We may find that the creative God challenges our categories and calls us to expand our minds and hearts. We can indeed be transformed by participating. And we thought we were just leading a theological reflection group.

I was fortunate to travel to the West Coast a few years ago. Because the flight back to the Midwest left early in the morning, several people on the plane promptly went to sleep shortly after takeoff. I had planned to do this as well. As we took off, however, the pilot announced that we could see Mount Rainier above the clouds if we looked off to the left. I was quite excited and turned to make sure the people across the aisle could see. They were sound asleep. As tired as I was, I was grateful to be awake to see the grandeur of this mountain. All the way home I kept pondering the blessing of staying awake because I got to see.

Theological reflection allows us the opportunity to see what we might otherwise miss. As leaders we provide an opportunity to see, but in the process we can delight in the revelation provided us. As we give to others, much is given to us. "Unless the Lord builds the house, those who build it labor in vain."

Ministers are busy people. Sometimes it can feel as if our lives are a blur. In the midst of our busyness we struggle to find time for personal reflection, knowing its importance. After all, we preach its importance. A young man in a theological reflection group I led remarked, "I want to be motivated, not driven." That comment captures the sense of centeredness that is required to live busy lives in a reflective mode.

Theological reflection affords us the opportunities to dive deeply, to surface, and to "walk on water." We know that even when we are not literally near water, we can still snorkel. We believe that the very air we breathe is the Spirit of the living God. We are convinced that what appears to be mundane has the power to be revelatory, if we but see (see *GDC*, #152–153). "Lord, that I may see."

For Reflection

1. In the morning read the Gospel for the day. What word, phrase, or image struck you? What in the reading resonated with you? At what point did you feel challenged? If you were to tell the message of the Gospel today, where would it be received with joy? Where would it be uncomfortably heard? Where would it be ignored?

2. In the evening, recall an experience from the day that had an effect on you. What were your feelings, concerns, questions, and delights? To which aspects of our Tradition do you feel a connection? a confrontation? If you were to tell Jesus about this experience, what would he say?

Abbreviations

CCC   *Catechism of the Catholic Church*

GDC   *General Directory for Catechesis*

RCIA   Rite of Christian Initiation of Adults

Bibliography

Catechism of the Catholic Church. Washington, DC: United States Catholic Conference, 1994.

Competency Based Certification Standards for Pastoral Ministers, Pastoral Associates and Parish Life Coordinators. Chicago: National Association for Lay Ministry, Inc. (NALM), 1994.

Coughlin, Kevin. *Finding God in Everyday Life.* New York: Paulist Press, 1981.

General Directory for Catechesis. Washington, DC: United States Catholic Conference, 1998.

Groome, Thomas. *Christian Religious Education: Sharing Our Story and Vision.* San Francisco: Harper and Row, 1980.

————. *Sharing Faith: A Comprehensive Approach to Religious Education and Pastoral Ministry.* San Francisco: Harper and Row, 1991.

Guzie, Tad. *The Book of Sacramental Basics.* Ramsey, NJ: Paulist Press, 1981.

Holmes, Urban. *To Speak of God: Theology for Beginners.* New York: Seabury Books, 1974.

Hug, James, ed. *Tracing the Spirit: Communities, Social Action, and Theological Reflection.* New York: Paulist Press, 1993.

Killen, Patricia O'Connell. *Journeys in Ministry.* Chicago: Loyola University Press, 1989.

Killen, Patricia O'Connell and John de Beer. *The Art of Theological Reflection.* New York: Crossroad, 1994.

Kinast, Robert. *Caring for Society: A Theological Interpretation of Lay Ministry.* Chicago: Thomas More Press, 1985.

————. *If Only You Recognize God's Gift: John's Gospel as an Illustration of Theological Reflection.* Grand Rapids, MI: Eerdmans, 1993.

————. *Let the Ministry Teach: A Handbook for Theological Reflection.* Maderia Beach, FL: Center for Theological Reflection, 1992.

National Certification Standards for Professional Parish Directors of Religious Education. Washington, DC: National Conference of Catechetical Leadership, 1998.

NFCYM Competency-Based Standards for the Coordinator of Youth Ministry. Washington, DC: National Federation for Catholic Youth Ministry, 1996.

Shea, John. *An Experience Named Spirit.* Chicago: Thomas More Press, 1983.

————. *The Spirit Master.* Chicago: Thomas More Press, 1987.

————. *Stories of God: An Unauthorized Biography.* Chicago: Thomas More Press, 1978.

Whitehead, Evelyn Eaton and James D. Whitehead. *Christian Life Patterns: The Psychological Challenges and Religious Invitations of Adult Life.* New York: Crossroad, 1992.

————. *Community of Faith: Models and Strategies for Developing Christian Communities.* New York: Seabury Press, 1982.

————. *Method in Ministry.* New York: Harper and Row, 1985.

Wingeier, Douglas E. *Working Out Your Own Beliefs: A Guide for Doing Your Own Theology.* Nashville, TN: Abingdon Press, 1980.

Recommended Resources

Books

Bausch, William J. *While You Were Gone: A Handbook for Returning Catholics and Those Thinking About It.* Mystic, CT: Twenty-Third Publications, 1994.

Brown, Raymond, Joseph Fitzmyer, and Roland Murphy, eds. *The New Jerome Biblical Commentary.* Englewood Cliffs, NJ: Prentice Hall, 1990.

Charpentier, Etienne. *How to Read the New Testament.* New York: Crossroad, 1987.

Greeley, Andrew M. *The Great Mysteries: An Essential Catechism.* New York: Seabury Press, 1976.

Myers, Susan. *Workbook for Lectors and Gospel Readers.* Chicago: Liturgy Training Publications, 1999. (Note that LTP provides this resource every year.)

Scagnelli, Peter J. *Sourcebook for Sundays and Seasons.* Chicago: Liturgy Training Publications, 1999. (Note that LTP provides this resource every year.)

Weber, Gerard P., and Robert Miller. *Breaking Open the Gospel of Luke.* Cincinnati: St. Anthony Messenger Press, 1990

Series

Ahern, Barnabas, Kathryn Sullivan, and William Heidt, eds. New Testament Reading Guide. Collegeville, MN: The Liturgical Press, 1963.

Duggan, Bob, Carol Gura, Rita Ferrone, Gael Gensler, Steve Lanza, Donna Steffen, Maureen Kelly. Foundations in Faith. Allen, TX: Resources for Christian Living, 1998. (Cycles A, B, C)

Karris, Robert, ed. Read and Pray. Chicago: Franciscan Herald Press, 1974.

——. Collegeville Bible Commentary. Collegeville, MN: The Liturgical Press, 1983.

Harington, Wilfrid and Donald Senior, eds. New Testament Message series. Wilmington, DE: Michael Glazier, Inc. 1979.

Powell, Karen Hinnan and Joseph Sinwell. Breaking Open the Word of God: Resources for Using the Lectionary for Catechesis in the RCIA. Ramsay, NJ: Paulist Press, Cycle A, 1986, Cycle B, 1987, Cycle C, 1988.

Catholic Update series. Cincinnati: St. Anthony Messenger Press.

Videos

The Faithful Revolution. Allen, TX: Resources for Christian Living, 1997.
Five one-hour videos and study guide.

Catholic Update series. Cincinnati: St. Anthony Messenger Press and Franciscan Communications.

Seeds of Faith. Westmont, IL: Sandlestrap Technologies, Inc., 1989.

Acknowledgments

Scripture citations are taken from the New Revised Standard Version
Bible, Catholic edition, copyright © 1993 and 1989 by the
Division of Christian Education of the National Council of the
Churches of Christ in the U.S.A. Used by permission. All rights
reserved.

The table on page 42 is adapted from the work of The Public
Conversations Project, National Study Circles Resources.

About the Author

Joye Gros, O.P., holds a Doctor of Ministry degree from St. Mary of the Lake University and a Master's in Religious Education from Seattle University. Her ministerial experience includes elementary education and service as director of religious education, and pastoral associate. Joye has both directed and trained directors and catechists for the Rite of Christian Initiation of Adults. Since 1992, she has served as an educational associate for Development in Ministry, Archdiocese of Chicago. She developed training programs for ministers of care, bereavement ministers, and catechists. Joye taught in the Diocese of Joliet Pastoral Leadership Program and facilitated the formation component of the Institute for Spiritual Companionship. She devotes high interest and energy to ministry formation, group facilitation, retreats, and days of reflection. Joye is a Dominican Sister of St. Catharine, Kentucky, and presently serves on her community's governing board.